WINDOW TO MY HEART

I used to ask God what lesson I had to learn
    before I could be rewarded with love.
I used to ask why I was undeserving.
I used to feel bitter,
        neglected,
        forgotten.

Sometimes I still look around and wonder,
    but I never doubt that
    His plan for my life is best.

WINDOW
TO MY
HEART

Reflections

of a single woman

JOY HAWKINS

LIVING BOOKS®
Tyndale House Publishers, Inc.
Wheaton, Illinois

Living Books is a registered trademark of Tyndale House
Publishers, Inc.

Front cover photo © Pat O'Hara
Interior illustration © Michael Hackett

Scripture quotations marked NIV are from the *Holy Bible,* New
International Version. Copyright © 1973, 1978, 1984 International
Bible Society. Used by permission of Zondervan Bible Publishers.

Library of Congress Catalog Card Number 91-65883
ISBN 0-8423-7977-0
© 1991 by Joy Hawkins
All rights reserved
Printed in the United States of America

98 97 96 95 94 93 92 91
 8   7   6   5   4   3   2   1

To Kim Abdo
Geri O'Donnell
Gina Miller
and Debbie Wager,
my friends who understand.

Carlton Pearson, thank you
for your teaching
and the example you set
for all singles.

CONTENTS

One
REALITIES
AND
RESOLUTIONS

WINDOW TO MY HEART

If you could see into the window of my heart,
you would see a huge, warm home,
    fire in the old, stone hearth,
    embroidered pillows on each chair,
    Appalachian wildflowers of every hue,
    handmade quilts, afghans, cross-stitch,
    smiling photographs of those I love,
    cinnamon rolls hot from the oven,
    room for all to enter, relax.
A strong sense of welcome,
    security,
    belonging
will meet you at the door.

Let me show you each sunlit room,
    each narrow hallway,
    each closet and stair,
    each award and souvenir,
    each scrapbook of memories,
    each dried rose petal and card.

This is my home.
This is my heart.
Always open to you.

HONEST EMOTIONS

Single.
Sounds simple.
But it's so complicated,
       so confusing.

Some people don't know how to treat me.
They don't know if I'm content or miserable.
They wonder whether this is my decision
       or if I'm brokenhearted.
They talk with me about love as if
       it is something I've never experienced.
They try to fix me up with their friends
       as if my heart is up for grabs.
They want me to have their life-styles,
       their remedy for happiness.
They mean well, but they really don't understand.

To be honest, I'm not sure I really understand either.
Sometimes I don't know how to act or respond.
I've been single all my life,
       and I still can't comprehend all the rules to the
       game.
Do I conceal my loneliness?
     Admit I'm content?
     Show my tears?
     Voice my frustrations?
     Reveal my peace?
Do I share with others all the contradictions
     I feel as a single woman?

Sometimes I dare not be vulnerable
        with my deepest feelings.
By opening up my soul, letting it
        speak for itself,
I often hear words that surprise even me.
Yesterday I was so content, so peaceful.
Now I hear my heart speak restlessness.
This morning as I planned my vacation
        I reveled in my freedom.
Now I dream of having someone special
        to share the memories with me.

I have all these feelings,
        all these honest emotions,
        all these hurts and joys.

I'm a single woman, discovering daily
        exactly what that means . . .
        to me.

NOW I'M READY

For several years I put my life on hold.
I bought few pieces of furniture,
    didn't start my doctorate,
    wouldn't commit to a two-year contract.
What if Mr. Right showed up
    and my pastel floral chairs
    didn't match his brown carpet?
What if he lived in another state,
    and my credits wouldn't transfer?
What if he didn't want a wife
    with long-term career goals?

I based each decision on an imaginary person.
He controlled my every move.
I wanted to make sure I'd be ready for him,
    adaptable to his needs,
    suitable for his taste in women.
I was putty waiting to be molded.
I was no one, eager to be told
    who I should become.

After many, many months of this
    aimless nonexistence,
I realized I have to be
    exactly who I am,
    who God created me to be.
I took my life off hold
    and started living.
I stretched my arms and reached for the stars,

hugged dreams,
and once again held self-respect close to me.

Now I'm more attractive
    because I have self-confidence.
I'm more interesting
    because I'm learning and
    growing each day.
I'm more exciting
    because I'm doing things
    and going places.
I'm more easygoing
    because I have peace.
I'm ready to meet my husband
    or even remain single
    because now I know who I am.

YOU'RE IN CONTROL

I don't know what brought on the tears.
It had been a fun evening with Cindy.
Dinner at the Italian restaurant,
      reminiscing about old flames.
Former boyfriends.
Men of our hearts.

I came home late. Tired from the day.
Quickly to bed, barely remembering to say,
      "Good-night, God. Thanks for my friend, Cindy."
As I pulled my pillow to me, I felt the sobs within.
Suddenly, uncontrollably, tears followed.
Emotions I didn't know I was feeling came forth.
Questions I hadn't asked for many months stirred
within.

"God, will I always be alone?
Will I ever again know a man's love?
Did You create me to stay single?
What do I do with all these feelings and desires?
Is this my permanent life-style?"

What brought on these tears,
      these questions?
I've been so happy lately,
      so content and fulfilled.
The thought of a relationship amid my busy schedule
      is overwhelming.
One of the two would suffer, and it can't be my career.

Men come and go.
My life continues.

I had myself believing that all is fine in my life.
And it has been.
But deep inside I know that I don't want to grow old
     alone.
It's a fear I try to hide even from myself.

I haven't lost hope.
I believe someday I'll marry.
But with each year I put on another layer of faux
     apathy,
          readying for the cold,
          preparing for my winter.

Lord, I don't know what made me cry.
It's just this heart of mine weeping,
     wondering what it's missing.
Deep inside my spirit, I really trust You.
Hold me close tonight.
Tell me one more time what I already know:
     You're in control.

DIVORCE

I'm blessed.
I've never committed my life
    to the "wrong" man.
Never felt a judge cut in two
    what God forever had joined together.
Never had to answer unanswerable questions
    for the children.
Never had to face society alone
    when before I'd always been part of a couple.
Never had to wonder if it was all my fault
    or if I'd given up too easily.
Never missed someone in my bed,
    sharing my intimate, daily life.
Never divorced.

Sometimes when I'm feeling sorry for myself,
    thinking about all the things I'm missing . . .
I stop and count my blessings.
I've missed the biggest heartbreak of all.

DINNER FOR ONE

The London Symphony Orchestra.
Candles.
Flowers.
My best dishes.
Dinner for one.

Sometimes I set the mood
    with music and flowers.
Fix my favorite recipe.
Light the candles.
And have a nice, quiet meal.
Alone.

No, I'm not pretending someone
    special is with me
    or even on his way.
And I'm not sad that he isn't.

I'm just a lady needing an evening
    with flowers, music, and candles.
Some call it a romantic evening.
And I've known it to be just that.
But not tonight.
Tonight it's just me.
No pretensions.
No expectations.
No fears of rejection.

Just me.
Satisfied to be alone this evening
    with the London Symphony Orchestra.

THE GUARANTEE

"If you travel, take classes, smile, have eye contact,
    and keep yourself looking attractive,
    you'll meet your husband."

"Will I?"

"Oh yes, it's guaranteed!"

"But I just flew in from a week in Chicago
    where I attended a conference to better myself.
    I've lost twelve pounds, and I wore all new, stylish
    suits and dresses. I smiled freely, always being
    careful to have eye contact. I won an award, made
    new friends, and toured museums—but I didn't
    meet him."

"Well, then, if you will get involved in church or
    community projects, change jobs, and let men
    know that you're interested, you'll meet him. It's
    guaranteed."

Lord, thanks for the peace in knowing that I don't
    have to strive or search to find Your perfect will for
    my life. All I have to do is trust You.
Then it's guaranteed.

FRUSTRATION

I feel so frustrated today.

My checkbook doesn't balance.
My car needs to be serviced.
My furniture needs to be moved.

I'm not incompetent
And I'm not lazy.
I'm a woman . . . a lady.
And I want to be treated special today.

I want a man to carry my luggage
        and argue with car salesmen
        and help make major decisions.

I feel so frustrated today.
I know how to take care of myself
        but I don't want to.

        Not today.

THE PROCESS

I used to feel that being single was shameful.
>   Like wearing a sign that says *rejected* or *failed*—
>   a type of scarlet letter for all to see.

I used to look at couples and wonder
>   what she did to deserve love.
And try to figure out
>   how they got together
>   and what attracted him to her.

I used to watch movies with happy endings
>   and cry from wishing it was like that for me.
And I'd read books about dreams coming true
>   and cry again.

I used to ask God what lesson I had to learn
>   before I could be rewarded with love,
I used to wonder why I was undeserving.
I used to feel bitter,
>   neglected,
>   forgotten.

I don't know when the moment of truth
>   or light was revealed to me.
I don't remember a time of suddenly
>   trusting Him to meet my needs.
It has been a process of tears,
>   long nights of prayer and questions,
>   and quiet moments of listening
>   to His voice.

Sometimes I still look around and wonder,
    but I never doubt that
      His plan for my life is best.

CONTENTMENT

I'm surrounded by married couples.
Some with children, some without.
Most have their own homes,
    others rent.
There are barbeques on
    Saturday evenings,
      weekends away in the country,
      and G. I. Joe birthday parties.
Milk is bought two gallons at a time,
    a cake is always in the oven,
      latest school papers on the fridge.
Dogs, cats, fish everywhere.

I can't relate to their life-style.
Unrealistic. Fairy tale.
I watch my friends move in and out
    of activities,
      plans,
      future goals,
    as if the whole world
    lives like them.
But I don't. It's all so foreign to me.

I've been single all my life.
It's all I know . . . my world.
And at times I'm envious
    as I watch my married friends.
There are obvious advantages to their lives.
I don't know the range of emotions

a woman feels during her wedding
    or upon hearing her child's first word
    or in planning her dream home.
I try to imagine these things sometimes.

But right now I'm single,
    living in an apartment,
    buying groceries,
    one bag each week.
My time is all my own,
    as are my decisions
    and my bills.
As in marriage, there are
    good and not-so-good days.
It's the only life I know.
And even though I watch
    and dream and wonder,
    I'm content right now
    just to be me . . .
    a single woman.

HIS PEACE

I didn't get the job.
I'm not sure I really wanted it,
    but I wanted it to be my choice.
I wanted them to realize my potential,
              appreciate my education,
              be impressed with my abilities.
But I didn't even get to the interview stage.
They rejected my resume. A mere piece of paper.

I joked when I told friends.
Said there are bigger and better things in store.
They agreed. Always on my side.
And I was fine till I went home.
Alone.
No one to tell me it's OK.
No one to talk it through with me.
No one to hold me.

Sometimes I love coming home
    to the solitude. Peace.
Sometimes I need someone
    waiting for me there.
Accepting me just the way I am.
Loving me anyway. Always.

Lord, I don't understand why
    I didn't get the job.
    I had the qualifications.
And Lord, I don't understand why

I'm not married.
I know I'd make a good wife.

But somewhere amid these
    questions and tears,
    I feel Your peace.
Amid the harsh realities of life
    I sense Your Spirit.
And I'm reminded once again
    that You know what is best
    for my life.
Today and tomorrow.
This very moment.

THE BATTLE

He took the form of loneliness
    and tried to steal my peace.
He placed within me a deep emptiness,
    a dark, cold cavern.
He whispered of being unlovable, undesirable.
He called out to me that there is no hope.
He cried of a life without companionship,
    old age without grandchildren.
He showed me mental pictures of happy couples,
    played me tapes of children's voices.
This loneliness is a murderer,
              a thief,
              a liar.

One day I took this loneliness
    to battle.
I quoted promises of God to me,
    words of hope and truth.
I proclaimed my trust in the One
    who died so that I would never be alone.
I spoke confidently of dreams and goals,
    my calling.
I replayed a life of contentment and peace.

I commanded loneliness to be gone,
    never to return.
I won the battle.

SAFE WITH YOU

I just got startled from a deep sleep.
Something kept rubbing against my window.
My heart jumped out of my bed,
        my body quickly followed.
Is someone trying to pry open the window?
Is the neighbor's cat playing night games
        in the bushes?
Is someone watching me right now as
        I sit with the light on?
I almost called the police, but I'd feel foolish
        if they found Prissy's eyes shining back
        at their flashlight.
I started to call my friend only miles away,
        but it's late, and I don't want to wake him.

Some nights it's real hard to be single
        and brave.
I don't own a gun or have a security system.
I'm just a normal, single young woman
        living alone.
And 99 percent of the time that's OK.
But tonight I feel scared.

When I was young I would scream for my dad.
He would come to my room,
        look in my closet
        peer under my bed,
He made sure everything was OK.

Then I could relax and go back to sleep.
I knew Dad was keeping me safe.

Now I'm silently screaming for You, Father God.
Whisper to me that everything is OK.
I'll turn out the light.
You're keeping me safe.

VIRTUOUS, NOT DOMESTIC

I'm not domestic,
    and I don't pretend to be.
I have no desire to ever cook
    a big Thanksgiving dinner and
    invite the whole family.
I've never had an urge to spend
    my morning out planting flowers
    and ruining my nails.
I buy wash-and-wear clothes,
    eat microwave popcorn for lunch,
    and let the Tidy Bowl man
    keep my toilet clean.

Don't get me wrong:
    I know how to cook.
I've done it before.
But it takes too much time
    to prepare meals and
    then clean them up.
And once I helped my mother
    set out a garden on our farm.
I even dug potatoes,
      picked strawberries,
      strung beans.

I'm not ignorant of domestic things.
There are just other things
    I'd rather be doing.
Things that are neat—

like reading or cross-stitch.
I learned a long time ago that
    the best way to keep
    a house looking clean is
    not to mess it up
    by cooking or ironing.

I get exhausted when I think
    about Proverbs 31.
Lord, when You created me,
    You made me someone special.
I'm virtuous in my own ways.
Just not domestic.

I'M JUST ME

Every time I come to the beach,
I can't help but notice all the slim women
    in their show-off suits.
And each time I vow—one more time—
    to go home and work out.

I'm not obese.
I look OK all dressed up.
But dress me down in a swimsuit and . . .
    what can I say?
Each love handle, stretch mark, broken vein—
    all of me shows.

I work hard at my job.
I don't want to come home and worry about
    calories and cholesterol.
I don't want to walk fast, ride bikes, or sweat.

I want to spend my days off at the pool
    or on this beach,
    relaxing, sunning,
    recharging my inner batteries.
But it's hard to relax when you have to
    hold in your stomach and keep your shoulders back.

I'm just me.
The one with the visor,
    a ponytail on top of my head,
    nose-coat protection,
    a one-piece suit.

No, I'm not surrounded by men
    or followed by whistles.
I'm just me. Snow Cone and all.
And I like me.
But tomorrow I need to start working out
    and dieting again.

Lord of this temple,
    help me to honor You
    in spirit,
        mind,
        and body.

STILL

I'm too old to act like this.
Too mature to giggle.
Too adult to cry.
So why all these emotions
    I felt as a child?
I try to act like a grown-up,
    but sometimes it's so hard.
I still love playing in the fallen leaves
    when I should be raking the yard.
I still love flirting with men that
    I know I'll never see again.
I still prefer my old jeans and sneakers
    over a sleek evening dress.
I still laugh out loud at things
    no one else thinks are funny.
I still cry, year after year, when
    the Grinch tries to steal Christmas.
I still get excited when it's my birthday
    and I know there's a special gift for me.
I still like singing songs in the car
    on long trips.
I still love my mom and dad
    and listen to their advice.
I still say my prayers at night
    before going to sleep.
I still fear God
    and wonder about heaven.

I still enjoy life here on earth.
I don't think I'll ever grow up.
I'm not sure I know how.

COOKING FOR ONE

I really hate to be at a women's social
    when someone focuses the conversation on
    cooking.
"My grandmother taught me how to make
cornbread."
"Well, my husband has never liked a meal without
meat."
"The cookbook was a wedding gift from his mother."
"Only Sandy can make homemade bread that good."
"Judy makes the best macaroni salad I've ever eaten!"
"I have to have the recipe for Jayne's broccoli soup."
On and on.

I sit there wondering if I should speak out about
    the great nachos I fixed last night.
Or maybe mention two Christmases ago
    when I made the banana-chocolate cakes.
One turned out OK.
I can make lasagna . . . and crab pasta salad
    and . . . hamburgers.
That's about it.

Cooking for one isn't worth the trouble.
I end up freezing most of it,
    or eating the same casserole
    for lunch and dinner all week.
I come in at 6:00 P.M..
No one is home expecting dinner.
Sometimes I stick a TV dinner in the oven

or pop some popcorn
or microwave leftovers.
Sometimes I just don't eat.
So I never practice cooking
or try out new recipes.
Why bother?

I think what I'll do is memorize a Betty Crocker
cookbook.
Then I'll join in . . .
"No, I always use a salt substitute."
"I prefer Gouda cheese melted on the vegetables."
"The best way to cook lamb is on 250, slowly."
Oh, I'd probably get all confused
and tell them that I bake Jell-O
for exactly fifty minutes
or describe a meal that would feed an army.
I've never been a good liar,
but I'm a worse cook.

Not cooking isn't so bad.
I seldom have pots and pans to scrub
or leftovers to throw out
and my grocery budget is so small
that I have money to eat out.

CLOSER

Sometimes I move my priorities around
    like a Rubik's cube,
Trying to get the right combination,
    the correct color scheme,
    the proper alignment.
Sometimes it gets so close . . .
    I'm successful at work.
    I'm dating a godly man.
    I'm keeping myself in shape.
    I'm staying within my budget.
    I'm growing spiritually.

I've almost solved the puzzle,
    almost put every block in order.
Then
    with the next move,
    one wrong turn,
    a piece is missing.
Or two are out of place.
And I'm back three moves,
    far from the desired outcome.

I need wisdom, Lord, every day.
Help me to know when it's time
    to change jobs,
    break off a relationship,
    make a commitment,
    invest in a risk.
I know You won't make

all the moves for me.
It's with each turn,
    whether right or wrong,
    that I learn more about Your will,
    and grow closer to You.

SINGLE-INCOME BUDGET

I'm on a single-income budget.
I can't pay an electric bill
    for twice the amount I anticipated.
I can't buy two new tires and also
    have a dental appointment
    in the same month.
Filling up the car with gas, getting a perm,
    buying an outfit, taking a trip . . .
    these are all planned events.
When I have to buy prescriptions or
    have my brakes repadded or
    make several long distance calls,
    my budget is ruined.
Impulsiveness was forced from my life
    the minute I started living on my own.

Dad told me this is good for me.
It forces me to learn the value of money.
It's kind of like being a child
    who has to eat liver and greens.
They're hard to swallow, but they make you grow
    strong.

All I know is that on months when there is
    a little left over, not only do I feel
    like I've accomplished something "mature"
    but I also feel like I deserve some ice cream.

THIS DESIRE

I think a lot about having a child.
Not as much as I used to, though.
I went through a stage in my mid-twenties
    when I was baby-crazy.
I watched babies intensely, amazed at their
    tiny, perfect bodies.
I loved to touch their skin,
    watch them smile in their sleep,
    let them wrap their small hands
    around my finger.
The desire to have a child was very strong.
I felt incomplete.
My heart ached.
I cried.
"Lord, what will I do without a child in my life?
    You put this desire in a woman's very soul.
    While growing up I always knew I'd be a mother.
    I feel deceived.
    Cheated.
    Empty."
But during the past couple of years I have come
    to understand and accept my life-style,
    though I did not choose it for myself.
I still love children.
Still wonder what it would feel like to be a mother.
Still dream.

For now I'm single,
        childless,
        and content.

A BALANCE

I don't like having to be strong
    all the time.
I'm a boss. A leader.
I deal with men as peers daily.
I have to act tough.
Keep a stiff chin.
Hide the tears.
Restrain the emotions.
Act masculine.

I'm trying to find a balance:
    leadership and femininity.
I'm a lady. Not one of the guys.
I'm strong.
But not as tough
    as I seem.

MY OWN SCHEDULE

It was one of those weekends.
No obligations.
No office work to finish.
It was even raining.
Perfect.

I put on my gown early Friday evening,
    popped popcorn and poured a Coke,
    then decided which book to read first.
A biography on Abraham Lincoln.
Although I was never interested
    in history during school,
    the older I become
    the more I want to know . . .
    about everything.
I waded through chapter after chapter
    on the Civil War.
By 2:00 A.M. my eyes would hardly open.
    I'd spilled the popcorn twice
    and finished two Cokes and one Snickers.
Rain rocked me to sleep until late morning.

Why get up?
I'll just pull the covers around my neck,
    arrange the other pillow to hold the book up,
    and start where I left off last night.
This mixture of laziness and academics
    continued through the afternoon
    till the book was finished.

A long, hot shower,
    a ham sandwich and a few chips—
    ready to begin the second book.
The sky had been dark all afternoon.
Hopefully my rain would return.

Lying on the couch, I entered a world
    of Southern ladies and their gentlemen.
    Plantations. Unrequited love.
Definitely more entertaining than Lincoln,
    though not brimming with facts to bring up
    in an intellectual discussion.
Evening melted into night
    as I completed the last chapter.
I was able to sleep securely knowing
    that Miss Ashley received her inheritance
    and won Jonathan's heart.

After church service the next morning,
    I had two days' dishes to wash,
    work clothes to iron,
    and some calls to return . . .
    but the escape was worth it.
My world is good, but every once in a while
    I want to travel away from reality,
    spend a weekend of solitude and rest,
    and be on my own schedule.
It's on weekends like this that
    I'm very thankful for singleness . . .
    and rain.

ON MY OWN

I never meant to be this age
    and still single.
I had my life planned out
    systematically.
Married by twenty-eight.
Children at thirty and thirty-two.
But it didn't go the way
    I'd planned.
I've been busy with my life.
Now I've woken up to find myself
    thirty-five and single.

You know, being thirty-five and single
    isn't so bad.
When I was in my twenties I was insecure
    and financially unstable.
I thought a woman couldn't make it
    on her own.
But I did, and I'm enjoying it.
I love coming and going as I please.
I love having the whole bed to myself.
I love not cooking if I don't want to.
I love deciding where I want to live.
I really do love being single at this age.

Two
ROMANCE:
ROSES
AND
REJECTION

STILL ALONE

Single bars with their
    artificial lights and moods
    lure the lonely, the seeking.
Laughter flows freely.
Conversations are light.
You can be whoever you want—
    find whatever you're looking for.
Until the morning hours close the doors.
You leave with a disappointed heart,
    with hair and clothes saturated with the
    nauseous smell of old smoke,
    with an emptiness that overflows.
Nothing has changed.
You face the next day still alone.
Still lonely.
Still seeking.

The Lord is close to the brokenhearted
and saves those who are crushed in spirit (Ps. 34:18, NIV).

I WISH

I wish you hadn't been my first love.
I wasn't ready to settle down.
Hadn't looked around enough to know
    what a treasure I'd found in you.
I couldn't make such a serious decision
    when I didn't know my choices.

It's been thirteen years since we said good-bye.
You've been married twelve.
I'm still single.
You've settled down,
    have your own business,
    the all-American family.
I've moved a hundred times,
    worked hard on my career,
    been in and out of relationships.
I can honestly say I've looked the whole world over
    and you're one of the best I've found.
A realization arrived too late.

I wish you had been more persistent.
I wish I had been more mature.

I'M SORRY

I thought it was real.
But I don't feel it anymore.
Maybe it was infatuation
    or love, short-lived.
I didn't mean to hurt you.
Didn't mean to make promises
    I can't keep now.
I can't pretend or play games
    with your heart.
Can't say I love you.
Just can't.

I'm usually on the receiving side
    of these words.
I've often been left standing,
    wondering what happened.
I know how it feels.
I'm sorry.

IMPOSSIBLE RELATIONSHIPS

She's thirty-two. He's twenty-three.
They're best friends.
Constant companions.
It started out like
    brother/sister.
They didn't intend
    to fall in love.

She's black. He's white.
They've worked together
    for years.
Always shared laughter,
    secrets, dreams.
Love came easily, secretly.
Though they've been warned,
    it's too late.

She's educated. He's not.
She was finishing her M.A.
    when they met.
Her car died on the interstate.
He drove the wrecker.
During the sixty-some mile drive,
    a spark ignited.

Impossible relationships.
Differences too obvious.
Social pressures unrelenting.
But they love each other.

Love is so hard to find
    in this world.
Some people never touch it.
Some find impossible relationships
    and make them possible.

TO OUTLAST THE MOUNTAINS

My grandmother was married in her mother's
    bedroom
    as her mother lay nursing her newborn child.
She had met my grandfather in church, and their
    courting
    consisted of the three-mile walk there each
    Sunday.
They had eleven children in the next twenty years.
Fed and housed on a coal miner's meager salary.
Surrounded by the strength and ruggedness
    of the West Virginia mountains.

My mother and father met in high school.
She was a cheerleader and he was the captain of the
    basketball team.
He used to come into the drugstore where she
    served ice cream and milk shakes.
He told everyone she was his wife. She laughed.
Then one cold December day they drove to Kentucky
    and eloped.
A small company house full of flowers and
    three daughters followed.

My sisters were both married in the same
    stained-glass Methodist church.
One's wedding was small, one's quite formal.
They have given me two nephews and one niece
    and marriages to emulate.

I used to plan my wedding with each serious
    relationship.
I changed colors and songs and bridesmaids as often
    as I changed prospective grooms.
I won't have eleven children. I doubt I'll ever elope
    or get married in that stained-glass church.
But someday if I marry I'll continue that same family
    determination to make a marriage work.
A commitment to outlast the mountains that bred my
    past.

YEARS OF PREPARATION

I love my job and can't believe it pays so well.
I like my apartment and my Honda.
I have friends who surround me with love.
I am blessed with a close family.
I have goals that keep me dreaming.
I have all a single woman could ever desire.
The best of life.

But sometimes I don't want to be a single woman.
I want a husband to love and encourage.
I want children to cuddle and teach.
I want to have cookouts with the neighbors.
I want to drive a station wagon with a dog in the back.
I want to go to PTA meetings and be a school
    volunteer.
I want to take a family vacation to Disney World.
I don't want to be so independent or self-sufficient.
I don't want to be alone.

Some married friends say they would trade life
    with me in a second.
They're tired, used up, and hungry for solitude.
If they had it to do over, they would never marry so
    young.

I'm thankful for all these years I've been single.
I've had time to find out who I am, what I want in life.
I've had time to search out my character.
I know my strengths and weaknesses.
I know I've got a lot to contribute.

I'm a woman who has been refined and defined
    by years of supporting and fighting for myself,
        years of sandpaper relationships,
        years of improving my abilities and talents,
        years of better understanding my moods,
        years of days and months as a single person
    now ready to be married.

THE BEST OF BOTH

When he came over the other night,
    I wasn't sure just how to act.
I was so afraid of seeming to be too forward,
    too interested,
    that I acted cool,
    distant,
    nonchalant.
I'm sure he left totally confused.
The previous night at the party
    I was attentive,
    focused on his every move,
    consuming each word he spoke.

Things have changed so much
    in the past decade for women.
We're supposed to be more assertive,
    more in control, leaders.
But I'm not quite sure how to take
    this attitude into a relationship.
I like having the car door opened for me,
    letting him take my coat,
    allowing him to drive.
I feel awkward making the first move,
    calling him just to talk,
    insisting that I pick up the tab.

It's confusing for both of us.
At work we're peers.

But when it comes to a personal relationship,
    everything changes.

I'm thankful for equal rights for women . . .
    to a point.
I guess I'm still hanging onto
    old-fashioned values.
Trying to have the best of both worlds.

HIS WAYS

He just called to say,
    "I'm on my way over."
Now I'm finishing my hair,
    checking my makeup,
    and thinking about changing clothes
    for the third time.
He'll have on khaki pants and a polo,
    damp hair from his shower—
    so predictable.
As he walks through the door he'll say,
    "Hi. How you doin' today?"
The same words he's been saying for the
    eleven months we've been dating.
I'll answer "fine" in the same tone of voice
    that I use for my dad,
    but with a different grin.

Thus ends the only ritual of our relationship.
The excitement I feel when he's near is fresh,
    day after day.
I look forward to each phone call at work,
    each scribbled note or card,
    each smile when he first sees me,
    each touch of his hand on mine.
Though he isn't a romantic,
    and roses are seldom sent my way,
    he always keeps my car in perfect condition,
    fixes things around my house,
    and goes with me to family gatherings.

Always consistent. Always there for me.
These are his ways of loving.

I wonder if I'll ever grow nonchalant with him.
I wonder if I'll ever tire of his dry sense of humor
    or his conservative way of thinking
    or his laid-back style of life.
Will I ever long for a man who talks stocks and bonds,
    wears expensive silk suits,
    and has read *Crime and Punishment*?
Sometimes I wonder.

Then he calls to say he'll be late for dinner
    because he stopped to change a tire for someone.
Or I hear the way he and my father talk about football.
Or I catch him staring at me in a crowded room.
Or I listen to him pray before a meal.

No, I'll never tire of this man.
I hope he never tires of me.

SO FAR APART

You're the closest person to me,
    yet we're so far apart.

One minute we're sharing laughter
    and stares and intimacies—
    our very souls.

Then, so quickly, with one sharp word
    or careless thought,
    we've put up a wall,
        shut a door,
          barred the other out.
    Unintentionally.
    Painfully.
    Regretfully.

But here we are again—
    so far apart.

Forgive me.

NOW I KNOW

We never fought or broke up.
It was a mind-over-heart decision,
        an act of our wills, not emotions.
And it was wise—best for both.

When you dropped by last night,
        we talked about old times—
        our times—good times.
You teased. I laughed.
We were both silent for long,
        comfortable seconds . . .
        remembering when.

You held my hand, rubbing each
        finger tenderly as we talked.
Reconfirming the attraction
        that began years ago.
How easy to slide back into
        a past relationship—
Like putting on my favorite old
        sweater on the first cool day
        of autumn.
It still fits just right.

I listened to the changes
        in your words and attitude.
I watched the way you walk
        with more confidence.
Things are different in your life:
        you earned a big promotion at work,

bought an expensive new car,
and put a down payment on a house.

When it was time for you to leave,
you gently kissed me good-bye.
It felt just like the kiss of the
uncomplicated, vulnerable young man
I loved years ago.

I used to wonder what you
would be like all grown-up.
Matured. Settled.
Now I know.

I couldn't sleep after you left.
I kept wondering if maybe
our hearts know best.

We've always been analytical,
relying on logic rather than emotions.
And our relationship has never been logical.
We are both so career-minded, so fast-paced.
How would we fit time for each other,
and possibly children, into our schedules?
But here we are, almost nine years later,
still in love.

SECURE IN OUR LOVE

We can wait.
We both felt we could.
So I took the job and
    moved far away.
Just for a year or two,
    three at the most.
If this is real, it will last:
    my final thought as
    I boarded the plane.
Neither of us felt in a hurry
    to marry, though we're not young.
Both of us felt secure in our love.

Long-distance love.
Letters promising,
    questioning,
    assuring.
Expensive phone calls
    repeating the same.
Heart-words full of emotion.

It's only been five months,
    yet I feel like
    we're becoming strangers.
How can mere pen and paper,
    rushed calls,
    keep us close?

In two short sentences you told me
    of your losing season.

A quick P.S. says
    you've had the flu.
"Oh, by the way . . ." lets me know
    you got that promotion at work.
It shouldn't be like this.
Our lives are becoming trivial—
    short, choppy phrases.

No, the love hasn't died.
That's why it hurts me
    to know you long-distance.
I want to be there for you.
I want to hold you close
    when a hug is what you need the most.
I want to listen to your coaching stories.
I want to watch you from the bleachers,
    feeling such pride that you're mine.
I want to be silent with you,
    secure in knowing that everything is OK.
I want to laugh at your jokes,
    smile at you across the room,
    hold your hand as we walk.
I want to be there daily with all the
    excitement, boredom, tears, laughter
    that belong to life.
I want to love you up close.

I'm coming home.

BRUISED BUT WISER

I knew what I was looking for in a man—
    settled, businesslike, financially stable.
    The *GQ* type. Wall Street's son.
When he sat beside me in church,
    I knew it was him:
    Northern accent, expensive cologne,
    Mercedes in the parking lot.
He was the desire of my heart granted.

Now it's two years later
    and the relationship is over.
I'm bruised but much wiser.
And thankful to still be single.

My eyes have been opened.
No longer will I be lured by an appearance
    that hides all the turmoil within.

And I have a new friend.
He's a dreamer, wears boots,
    drives a pickup,
    and has a Southern drawl.
    Looks like the Marlboro man.
Not my type at all,
    but I'm drawn to his gentleness,
    the quiet way he moves through life.

God, I'm so glad my heart is in Your hands.

I THOUGHT WRONG

I offer you a listening ear,
           open arms,
           a heart that cares.
I justify your wrongs,
     soothe your aches,
     kiss your wounds.
I believe in your dreams,
     even make them my own.
I learn your subjects,
     talk your talk.
I'm proud to be by your side
     and pretend it's where I belong.

Why did I get myself into
     this hopeless relationship?
I have this bad habit
     of looking past reality
     and finding potential in each person,
     especially a man.
I saw you as all the things I need,
     all the things I desire
     in a husband.
And I know you can be all these things.
The loyalty, sensitivity, honesty—
     it's all there: deep inside the shell,
     hiding behind the little boy smile,
     underneath the layers of pride,
     next to the walls of fear.

It's all there . . . and I can help find it,
    draw it out.
So I thought.

LIKE US

It has been almost a year
 since things got crazy
 and we broke up.
"Broke up"—it sounds so juvenile
 yet describes it perfectly.

Like a pot carefully turned
 on the wheel,
 smoothed and pressed
 into the desired form.
It looked durable, strong.
 But once the pot
 was placed in the kiln,
 the fire found a weak area,
 too thin to withstand
 the pressure of the heat.
And the pot cracked,
 breaking into two hard pieces.

Like us.

Master Potter, forgive us
 for trying to make pots
 of our own desire and form.
Only You can create relationships
 that endure fire.

HEAL MY BROKEN HEART

I know what a broken heart feels like.
I know this feeling well.
When I was a child, it took little
    to break my heart—
    a lost toy, a word of rebuke,
    a teasing friend.
Now the pain is deeper
    and lasts longer than a day.

It's like coming out of an accident
    with no visible cuts or broken bones,
    just internal bleeding
    and bruises that last a long time.
I can't stitch it up
    or put a Band-Aid on it.
A cast won't help it mend.
So I pop painkillers—
    one called apathy, another pity.
And I go on
    pretending I don't hurt,
    fooling no one.

Lord, right now my heart
    feels so small, so torn,
    so childlike.
I let someone get too close to it.
To be honest, I placed it
    right into his hands.
I trusted him to hold it near,

to treasure the most precious gift
    I could give him.
But his hands were rough and calloused,
    unaccustomed to such a fragile possession.
He often dropped it carelessly
    or laid it down without thought.
And I let him.
Never asking for it back.
Always hoping, always believing.

Healer of broken hearts,
    can You mend mine
    one more time?

YOU'RE DIFFERENT

You say you love me,
 and sometimes I almost
 believe you.

You walked into my life
 when a relationship
 was not my desire.
I had my walls up
 for protection.
I still do.
But you're so patient,
 not trying to tear them down.
You let me choose
 when to remove a layer
 or one brick at a time.
You're vulnerable with me,
 never insisting I be the same.
I've pushed you back,
 stood you up,
 denied my feelings.
Yet you're still here.
Waiting on my timing . . .
Waiting on my heart.

Tell me this isn't a game
 like the last one.
He pursued my affections,
 required my devotion,
 insisted on transparency.

And I gave my all so freely,
      with nothing in return.
When he walked away smiling,
      having built up his ego,
      I swore to never love again.
Never again to be a trophy
      for a game well played.
Never again to be so foolish.
Never again to be in love.

Now here you are.
Saying that you're different.
Seeming to be so sincere, so committed.
Telling me you love me.

My heart is tender.
My emotions so fragile.
Please be gentle.
Please be honest.
Please love me.

WITHOUT THEM

I don't need a man
    to make me complete.

I don't need a man
    to give my life meaning.

I don't even need a man
    to provide financial security.

But . . . I love the feeling
    of being loved by a man.
    Appreciated. Respected.
    Cherished. Needed.

I've known men in my life
    whose smile could eradicate
    my exhaustion or worries
    from a hard day at work.
Their simple touch or kiss
    could work miracles for my
    self-esteem.
The sound of their voice in a
    late-night call could warm
    me in the chilliest season.

No, I don't need a man
    to come into my life
    and change my identity
    or surround me with security.

But life would sure be dull without them.

Three
RELATIONSHIPS

KEEP LOVING ME

I never wondered what it would be like
    growing up without you.
I never had to.
You sat in the front row of
    each recital and performance.
You were officers in the PTA and
    Band Parents' Association.
You clapped louder than other parents
    at the school plays.
You respected and encouraged my
    creativity in writing and art.
You let me be me, whoever that was,
    at each stage of my life.

When I was in grade school,
    you let me voice my questions and my anger
    over the riots I saw on TV.
When I was in junior high school,
    you let me wear a ring on each finger,
    a POW bracelet, and clothes
    I made myself.
When I was in high school,
    you drove me almost daily
    to all the extracurricular activities
    in the evenings.
When I was in college,
    you gave me freedom to change my major each
    semester and backpack through Europe.

I haven't always made good grades.
I haven't always dated men you liked.
I haven't always made the right decisions.
I haven't always chosen the correct road
    to travel down.
You've been disappointed, angry, fearful,
    sad, and hurt.
But you've never stopped loving me.

Now that I'm older, we're more friends
    than parents and daughter.
But I still need your wisdom, your love.

Keep loving me through the stages
    of my life.
I may not be a child anymore,
    but I'm still growing.

GOD'S MAN

My dad is so sensitive.
His feelings run deep.
His tears flow freely.
His laughter is contagious.

He has taught me so much about
        honesty and vulnerability.
He has shown me that sincerity
        should show in my eyes,
        love in my smile.
He has told me that it's OK
        to be emotional
        as long as the emotions
        are from the heart.
He has shown me that living
        a gentle, caring life
        is always best.

He is a real man.
God's man.
I'm reminded of that
        each time I see
        his tears and his smile.

A FATHER LIKE YOU

When I was three you dressed me
    in a bow tie and skirt when we went to church.
When I was four we watched wrestling on TV together.
When I was five I used to sneak out of our house
    when Mom fell asleep during my nap time.
I would run up the road to your office across the bridge.
"Look, Dad! A present for you!" I emptied my pockets
    of grasshoppers, frogs, and worms.
When I was six you walked me to school.
No more sharing lunches and midday laughter.
When I was seven you gave me a train,
    eight, an erector set,
    nine, a basketball and hoop.
Thus I grew up, jokingly called your "only son."
We moved furniture, painted, took walks in the park,
    and laughed for hours.
Always a special bond.

As I matured, and makeup became my style,
    you encouraged me to become a proper young lady.
You taught me right from wrong by your example.
You made me feel worthy of the best life had to offer.
You sacrificed for my education, trips abroad, my car.
Your "son" became the daughter of your heart.

There is one thing you never told me, Dad:
How will I ever find a husband
    who can be a father just like you?

OPEN HEARTS

Mom and I had a long talk
    the other day.
It's the first time
    that I've pulled myself
    out of the daughter role
    to face her—
    woman to woman.

My words were bold, poignant, honest.
Each one spoken brought more freedom
    to speak yet another.
We talked of family trials,
    misunderstandings,
    broken relationships.
Each sharing blame,
Each seeing new light.

Two open hearts
    finding healing.

A MOTHER'S HEART

A call came to the church.
"Can someone keep my baby?
I've been kicked out of my home.
I can't take care of him right now."
The voice was frantic, a stranger
    to us all.
But we care for the homeless,
    the fatherless, the unloved.
The receptionist said my name
    immediately came to mind.
I agreed to go pick up the newborn.

The parents needed a miracle—
    a healing of their marriage—
    so I kept their son
    for five weeks.
Dark skin, large searching eyes,
    full of baby sounds.
I took him into my home.
He smiled his way into my heart.

Juggling a job and a newborn
    is exhausting.
Feedings every three hours.
Bottles to boil.
Formula to prepare.
Diapers and more diapers
    to change.
Baby baths. Baby coos.

My borrowed son was hard work
and wonderful.

He's back with his mom now
and his dad.
I'm praying they stay together.
Praying that all my prayers
spoken for him during his
night feedings are answered.

Lord, as Andrew bonded to my heart,
bond him to Yours.
Be there with him as he learns to walk
through life.
Be his Father, if his leaves again.
Be his Friend, when one is hard to find.
Be his Lord, when he's old enough to choose.

Thank You for loaning me this child.
I found that deep within this single heart
is a mother's heart . . . just waiting.

LIKE MY OWN

My sisters' children
    are like my own.
My sisters would laugh
    if they heard me say that.

"Then you can sit up with them
    at night when they're ill."

"Are you going to help us
    put them through college?"

"Will you keep them
    during the summer months?"

Well, they're kinda
    like my own.
I guess I get some of the
    benefits of having children
    without the responsibilities.
I cheer at their ballgames,
    clap at their recitals,
    cry at their graduations.
I give advice on dating,
    take pictures before proms,
    buy them special things.

No, I haven't held them till
    their fevers broke,
    or wiped their tears when
    someone hurt their feelings.
I don't know the daily energy

and patience needed to raise
these children.
I don't understand the selflessness
of buying for them first.
I can't relate to the laughter,
fights, talks, tears, and pride
that are all a part of having children.

I admire my sisters
and love their children
as my very own.

DON'T RUSH

You're sixteen.
You've traded in your dolls
    for a boyfriend.
You've decided on a career
    in fashion design.
You're driving,
    learning to be more independent.
You're smart, decisive, witty.
Heading full force into
    the twenty-first century.

Things are moving too fast,
    high-tech magnified.
So much is expected of you,
    so much will be demanded.
The pressure to be it all:
    the devoted wife,
    the loving mother,
    the assertive businesswoman,
    the community leader.
A simple life will be hard to find.

Alisha, in your rush to grow up,
    to experience it all,
    don't let go of His hand.
The world is telling you
    that the abnormal is normal,
    that you have the right to
    kill your unborn children,

that divorce is easy,
that you have to climb the
corporate ladder to succeed.
Opportunities
and options
and opinions will rush at you.
Be wise. Be true to yourself.
Be faithful to His Word.

NEVER ON MY OWN

I wanted to move far away
    from my family and friends.
Just for a year or two.
I wanted to be an adult on my own.
Learn more responsibility,
    become individually secure
    and self-reliant.
I've always felt so protected.
There was always someone to run to
    if things got too bad
    or something broke.
So I moved continents away
    to live alone among strangers.

But I'm not alone.
It seems no matter where I go
    I always find family,
    people who draw me into their arms.
So, it may not be Dad fixing the drain,
    or it may not be Rita asking me to dinner,
    but someone is.

I moved thousands of miles away
    to learn and grow
    and I am . . .
    yet I'm still among family.

If I take the wings of the dawn,
If I dwell in the remotest part
of the sea,
Even there Thy hand will lead me" (Ps. 139:9-10).

BEST FRIENDS

You're my best friend,
    whatever that means at our age.
I've tried to pinpoint what makes
    us close.
Our common faith?
Our single status?
Our chosen profession?
Maybe.
But I think it's probably
    just loyalty.
We stick by each other.
We each decided a long time ago
    to make this friendship work,
    no matter what.
There have been times when that
    wasn't so easy.
But we've hit a point where
    we accept each other
    exactly as we are.
No excuses. No trying
    to change the other.
It's a marriage of sorts:
    best friends.

FORGIVENESS

I didn't mean to say it.
It just came out unexpectedly.
I told her I would keep it quiet.
And I fully intended to protect her secret.

I don't know what made me say it
    or even think about her heart's dark corner.
I knew the moment it was out that
    I had probably lost my friend,
    hurt her irreparably.
No amount of apologies could erase
    the words I'd carelessly spoken.

I rushed to tell her what I'd done
    before she heard it on the street.
"I'm so sorry. You trusted me with your past,
    and I abused that confidence."
I cried. She sat quietly for several minutes.
Then, as if in slow motion, she walked to me,
    bent by my chair and touched my arm.
"It's OK. Your tears reveal your heart.
    I forgive you."

That forgiveness was the cement of our
    friendship for years to come.

MY EXTENDED FAMILY

I never wanted another roommate.
I had said several times that my next move
    would be into a house with a husband.
I was tired of sharing my life and my home
    with other females.
I wanted my furniture and my pictures
    where I wanted them.
No more mixing contemporary with traditional.
No more compromising about where the plants
    would go.
No more juggling of my schedule around a
    roommate's plans.
No more sitting in a bedroom all evening for some
    privacy.
No more roommates.
No more.

Private tears were shed as I moved all my
    belongings into your home.
The cost of living alone had once again
    forced me into an undesired decision.
It wasn't that I disliked you or your house.
You had become one of my close friends,
    and I already had spent many evenings at your
    home.
It was just the thought that I was nearly thirty
    and still living with roommates . . .
    another year of "dorm life" when
    it was time to be a wife.

Your home became my home for nearly two years
    until a job called me to another city.
There were few tough times sharing one house.
We both compromised, rescheduled, rearranged.
I'm allergic to pine, and although you hate fake
Christmas trees,
    you decorated ours beautifully with gold ribbons.
I was in and out of a painful relationship,
    and you tolerated his visits and my tears.
You like things immaculate and coordinated
    but lived with my travel posters, angel collection,
    word processor on the table, and garage full of
    books.
You taught me how to shop for bargains,
    whether I needed the item or not.
You showed me that it's possible
    to pay off credit cards monthly.
You let me love your daughter
    as I would my own.

The two of you became my extended family:
    my sister, my daughter.
And although it wasn't a situation
    I would have chosen,
It was obviously one ordained by my Father.

ROOMMATE

I've used your makeup,
    borrowed your clothes,
    typed your papers.
I've invaded your privacy,
    kept you awake,
    made you listen.

You've made me eat bran,
    forced me to jog,
    taught me to cook.
You've cried on my shoulder,
    borrowed my money,
    introduced me to Renoir.

We've shopped, binged, exercised.
We've walked on the beach before sunrise,
    shared secrets and fears till 2:00 A.M.,
    cried when the other was hurt.
We've encouraged each other's faith,
    sang songs with the radio,
    double-dated with only one man.
We've always been there for each other.

You're my friend.
You're like my sister.
You're my roommate.

BOTH OF US

You've divorced twice,
    have a daughter from each marriage.
I'm single, never married,
    no children.
We go through such different emotions.
Have such different problems.
Yet somehow our paths crossed
    and our hearts bonded.
You've opened my eyes to how
    life can be as a single woman.

I reassure you that you're
    a great mother.
You tell me that being single
    isn't so bad.
I listen to your frustrations
    of late child-support checks,
    your fears of raising children
    without a father's guidance.
You listen as I tell you
    my frustrations of broken
    promises and evenings alone.

I'm glad you finally received
    that promotion at work
    and got rid of that old car.
You're proud of me for winning
    the writing contest,

losing weight,
and ending a senseless relationship.

We both dream of life differently,
yet we've both found contentment
in our lives.
We're different,
but so alike.

INHERITANCE

*Sons are a heritage from the Lord, children a reward from
him (Ps. 127:3,* NIV).

The framed verse above the crib
    seemed to set the attitude of the nursery.
Their tiny boy, the image of his father,
    lay sleeping on the pastel blanket.
She touched his curled fingers as if
    counting them once again.
He wound the music box in the cotton lamb,
    and "Jesus Loves Me" softly filled the room
    with reverence and joy.
The child's inheritance encompassed him,
    cocoon-like in its security.
I watched from the door
    and pondered this miracle.

As I left the apartment, I felt
    I was saying good-bye to my old friends forever.
We had shared spring breaks, college books,
    future dreams, our faith.
But now they were going
    on a journey all their own.

Lord of this little family,
    will I ever travel
    down this road?

OUT OF CONTROL

My friend is having an affair.
Such a shallow, weak word.

The man is much older, a leader,
    and obviously unhappily married—
    like my friend.

My friend said that she and her husband
    have grown apart.
The communication was strained when he lost his job
    and she was supporting them.
When things were nearly silent
    and she was really lonely,
    the other man appeared,
              listened,
              understood.

Now it's out of control.
How do you stop a fire from spreading
    when a sudden breeze rushes through
    dry and thirsty woods?

I have such a hard time understanding marriages—
    especially unhappy ones.
Isn't it a commitment that you choose,
    an institution ordained of God,
    a union of two in love?
Maybe that's just the terminology.
In reality it's different,

not so holy or so loving.
Or so it seems today.

My friend is having an affair.
And she's torn.
Bonded to two.
Happy-sad.
Scared.
Guilty.

My friend is having an affair.
And all I can do is listen,
                        pray.

HER HEART

Yes, I know we're different,
    but she's my close friend,
    one of my dearest friends.

I love to hear her stories.
She's so animated,
    so verbally colorful.
When she talks, I listen.
And laugh till I cry.

I love to watch her with people.
She touches when she talks,
    drawing some near, turning some off.
Her vocabulary is vulnerable, open,
    at times offensive to the less open.
And she always steals the show—
    the life of the party.

Her eyes reflect her love of life,
    her exuberant spirit, her heart.
What a heart!
When she loves, she loves deeply, loudly . . .
    whether it be her husband, Bill,
                her dog, Max,
                her students,
                her God.

God, I know You must really love her, too.
You created her.
You know her best.

Thank You for my friend.
She says so many things that
    I can't find the words to express.
She makes our every meeting a fiesta.
She gives me so much of herself.
She makes me feel special.

Yes, I know she's different.
But she's burrowed into my heart
    and I want her to stay.

A SPECIAL GIFT

Chicago is a big city
    but not too big for you.
You speak of things that most women
    never contemplate.
You step into the male world daily
    and earn respect.
You demand the best from those around you—
    your students, friends, peers.
You're strong. Nearly invincible.

But when we talk I hear the compassion
    in your voice. You care.
You're gentle with my feelings
    and handle them with sensitivity.
You're emotionally what I need
    in a friend.
You're the one who keeps our friendship
    going strong . . .
    across the miles,
    bridging the races,
    throughout the years.

I admire your toughness.
I appreciate your gentleness.
God gave me a special gift
    in you.

Four
REDEEMER

YOU UNDERSTAND

You were 100 percent man while living on earth.
     And 100 percent God.
I'll never understand that paradox,
     but I know it to be truth.
You took upon Yourself the flesh of man,
     with our emotions and temptations.
You went to school and learned a trade.
You worked hard each day to make a living.
You watched as Your friends got married
     and started their own families.
You lived alone most of Your adult years.
Your family became those who surrounded You
     wherever You were traveling.

Were You lonely at times, even among friends?
Did You long for someone to hold You close
     after a hard day of being misunderstood?
Did You want someone to listen
     to the intimate thoughts of Your heart?
Did You ever watch children and feel cheated?
Did You ever ponder the desires of the flesh
     as a single man?
Did You ever daydream of life differently?

You understand, don't You, Lord?

PERFECT LOVE

Lord,
> You never wooed me
> or enticed me
> or overpowered me.
> You never made promises
> You couldn't keep.
> You never talked me
> into loving You.
> You never had to.

> You were patient
> and understanding
> as I submitted to
> Your sovereignty.
> You only came when
> invited and welcomed.
> You found pleasure
> in pleasing me.

> You have consumed
> all of me, as
> no man ever could.
> I let You.
> I love You.

MY STABILITY

My convictions run deep.
My standards are set high.
My beliefs are secure after
    years of seeking.
I know who I am.
I know what I'm after.
I even understand my purpose
    in this journey we call life.
I'm bold.
I'm confident.
I'm so honest that I often
    get myself into trouble.

Yet sometimes I feel like
    such a wishy-washy woman.
My emotions can soar and dip
    in mad extremes within minutes,
    possibly seconds.
New dreams and ideas bombard
    my every thought,
Leaving me wondering if that
    was my voice I just heard.

The conversation was light and
    my opinion was asked about
    something rather generic.
I listened as words
    stumbled out.
The answer was unimportant

but it left me questioning
        if I really know
        or understand my inner self.
Yesterday I would have answered
        much differently than today.
Tomorrow, what will I say?

I know that a double-minded man
        is unstable in all his ways.
But I don't feel unstable.
I feel like I'm growing,
        gaining fresh insight,
        learning from new experiences.
And sometimes all these changes
        in my life and mind are so fast,
I feel like I'm spinning in circles.
My thoughts and words become strangers
        even to me.

Lord, keep me open to the working
        of Your Spirit within me.
Be my stability during each stage
        of my metamorphosis.

HIS PRESENCE

I started feeling ill and
    went to bed around noon.
What a way to spend a Saturday.
I had plans of shopping and
    catching a movie matinee.
I kept waking up hot, cold, hot,
    unaware of the hours lost to sleep.
I awoke once as the evening sun barely
    lit my room, my sheets in tangles,
    one pillow on the floor.
I'm really ill—the reality hit.
And alone in a strange town.

In all my months of business travel,
    I had never faced illness alone.
I'd been lonely, bored, exhausted,
    but never had I felt so sick.
Calling a friend or parent, states
    away, would do no good.
I tried to think of what I should do.
I didn't feel the fever and aches
    warranted the emergency room.
Or did they?
I'd always had a second opinion
    on these matters.
I barely had the energy to call
    room service for a Coke.
      The thought of food nauseated me.
Should I tell the boy I'm ill?

What could he do?
I took some aspirin with the drink,
    seeking some instant cure,
    hoping for relief.
How could one body ache this badly?
How could I be so ill, so alone?

Finally in my desperation, tears
    mixing with my feverish dampness,
    I called out for the only
    Help I knew.

Sleep encompassed me all during the night.
When I awoke, I barely remembered the day before.
A little weak, hair hanging in my face, I walked
    to the shower thinking only of breakfast.
As steaming water cleansed reminders of the
    fever from my body, my heart remembered
    His presence during the night.
God had never left my room.
As a mother cares for her ill child,
    so He had cared for me.

Lord, thank You for healing me,
    for loving me,
    for never leaving me all alone.

TOGETHER

Lord, is it OK if we don't talk today?
Can we just be?
Can my thoughts be my prayers?
Can my desire to be in Your presence
    be my worship?

This week has been so smothering,
                    so confining.
I'm weary of talk, tired of doing.

Our silence together is comfortable,
                    comforting.
I'm content with You
Just to be.

WHISPER PEACE

God, sometimes I feel so scared
　　that I'm not doing enough
　　to earn You in my life.
I guess it's the American work ethic
　　I've learned so well.
I would never expect to win my living
　　through the lottery.
And I could never expect a God like You
　　to love me—simple me—
　　without reason.

For many years I worked hard to be worthy of You.
I paid my tithes,
　　went to church three times a week,
　　prayed and studied the Bible,
　　witnessed to my friends,
　　taught Sunday School,
　　even did missionary work.
I knew all the right terminology to sound spiritual.
And I loved You.
I loved You and would have done anything
　　to assure my position in Your kingdom.

But I got tired, God.
Exhausted. Used up.
Much of the joy was gone.
　　Only rituals, legalism, and striving
　　to be Your child remained.
So I pulled away.

Not from You,
   but from all the works.

This past year has been quiet,
   and at times I've felt scared
   that I'm not doing enough for You.
I still live by Your teachings,
   still listen to Your voice.
But there's no striving.
I've gone back to the basics: love, joy, faith, peace.
I like this feeling of being in Your arms—
   resting, listening—
   instead of running ahead of You
   to do Your work, Your will.

So God, when I get scared
   that I'm becoming lukewarm,
   whisper peace to me once more.
Remind me that I can do nothing to earn You.

You are a gift.

THIS CLOSE

Security surrounds me today, Lord.
I feel Your big arms
    drawing me even closer to You.
I can rest, relax,
    knowing this is where I belong.
This close to You, Lord.

Tomorrow I may pull away some.
Yesterday I did.
I made plans without prayer.
I spoke words without thought.
I was inconsistent,
    independent.
I was wrong.

But today I'm close to Your voice,
        secure in Your arms,
        where I belong.

I NEED YOU

Lord, I need You.
After midnight when I'm afraid
    from night sounds
    and my imagination has created more fears,
I visualize Your angels guarding my house.
Invisible protection.
And I quote Psalms until falling asleep.

Lord, I need You.
When the figures and fast talk of salesmen
    have me going in circles of confusion
    and a decision must be made—
I walk away from the situation
    to find out what You want me to do.
I do all the talking. You just listen.
Things seem to be so much clearer in Your presence.
Soon I have the wisdom I need.

Lord, I need You.
When I'm waiting in the mall on my friend,
    I always sit and watch the people.
It sure seems there are a lot of couples in love.
I feel lonely. Uninvited to society's party.
Then You're right there by my side,
    holding me close,
    whispering sweet promises
    for my future.
When my friend finally arrives,

she thinks I'm alone.
But I never am.

Lord, I need You.
When it seems my days and nights
    are consumed by trivial things,
    and I'm smothered by the small talk,
    gossip, and shallowness of the world.
I feel dirty, empty.
I have to get away from it all
    and run to You.
Only You can make me feel clean again.
Only You can fill me with peace.
I sing songs of praise,
    I joy in Your presence.

Lord, thanks for always being there
    when I need You.

CALM MY NERVES

Last year I was on a flight
    that quickly lost altitude.
I felt like I was in a toy
    being dropped carelessly by a child
    to the pavement.
Our hot trays of food
    levitated to the ceiling.
Soda cans rolled and spewed up and down the aisles.
People were on top
    of nearby strangers.
The stewardess was hurt,
    glasses were broken,
    clothes were stained.
I can still picture it all
    in my mind.
For those few seconds
    of fast free-fall,
I felt closer to death
    than ever before.

Now, after years of travel,
    I'm afraid of flying.
When the plane rocks and jerks
    over the Atlantic or Sahara,
    I feel overcome with fear.
Not fear of dying.
I'm anxious to be with my Lord.
But I'm afraid of the act
    of death itself.

It's an emotion I can't control.
A battle I can't seem to win.

God, calm my nerves,
    ease my fear.
I trust You with my life
    in all other circumstances.
Help me to trust You
    when I travel by air.

COMMISSION

I'm in awe of Your presence
    when You fill my room or thoughts.
I want to cry out as Isaiah did,
    "I'm unclean!"
But before the words are uttered
    You've baptized me in Your holiness,
    You've clothed me in new garments,
    You've filled my lips with praise,
    You've brought me into the Holy of Holies.

Your presence brings
    a sweet completeness,
    a calm fulfillment,
    a peaceful rest,
    a new commission.

Here am I.
Send me.

COMMUNION

No waves.
A penetrating quiet.
A see-through stillness.
A lonesome seagull beacons me
    to wade the warm Gulf waters.
Tranquil communion.
The Creator and I are one.

WAITING

Lord, help me to hold on
    to Your promises.
Help me to wait on Your will.

I don't want to be like Abraham.
You promised an heir.
You never lie.
But he got impatient and
    took the situation into
    his own hands.
And I don't want to be like Rebekah.
She knew Jacob would receive the blessing,
    the inheritance of Isaac.
Yet she schemed and deceived
    to make it happen right then.

Lord, was it their lack of faith?
    Was it their human nature?

Sometimes it does seem so much easier
    to take things into my own hands,
    my own timing, my own will.
I get tired of waiting.
Tired of being so patient.

Slow me down, Lord.
Help me to see things
    with Your eyes.

An eternal perspective.
A calm abiding.
A sure trust.

YOUR VOICE

Several years ago I thought
    I heard Your voice.
Clearly.
Loudly.

I acted upon the words.
Spoke out in faith.
Fully trusting,
    believing.

But I was wrong,
        misguided.

Confusion followed.
Hurt.
Fear.
Distance.

Lord, I know You speak
    to Your children.
I want to be like Samuel
    and listen for Your voice.
Discerning man's words
    from Yours.
And I want to be like Elijah
    when he was in the cave.
He wasn't moved by the
      strong wind
      or earthquake
      or even fire,

but by a tiny whisper—
Your still, small voice.
Like David, let me say,
    "When I call out
    to the Lord,
    He answers me from
    His holy hill."

No, I'm not a prophet.
I'm just a simple woman,
        a school principal,
        a weaver of words,
        a believer in You.
Ready once more to listen.
Drawing closer to Your heart,
    closer to Your voice.
Whisper, Lord.
I'm listening,
    waiting.

NOT ALWAYS

Lord,
I'm not always
    trustworthy.
I've misused precious gifts
    You've given to me.

I'm not always
    faithful.
I've knowingly placed
    other gods before You.

I'm not always
    self-controlled.
I've compromised
    my standards and beliefs.

I'm not always
    honest.
I've made vows to You,
    then done the opposite.

I'm not always
    giving.
I've become selfish
    with my time.

I'm not always
    forgiving.
I've waited for
    an apology.

I'm not always
  loving.
I've spoken words
  that were unkind.

But, Lord, I'm trying.
I want to be like You.
Help me to change.

LADY OF HIS

Lady of freedom,
    what have you learned during these months of
    unrestraint?

Lady of tears,
    how much hurt can one soul endure till it grows
    numb?

Lady of love,
    in pouring out the depths of your heart, was the
    love returned?

Lady of His,
    are you coming home bruised and weak and wiser?

SEND ME

Lord, I don't understand.
I know I was following Your leading.
I know I heard Your call to missions.
So I interrupted my career,
     left all that was familiar,
     put a relationship on hold.
And I came to this African country.
For You.

Yes, I admit I was also lured
     by a sense of adventure.
But that's OK, isn't it?
It's that part of my personality
     that makes me ready to go
     when I hear You speak.
So here I am, fighting mosquitoes,
                    healing from hepatitis,
                    preparing for an evacuation.

It's hard for me to see what good I've done
     for You and the great commission.
Have I been a light?
Have I lived Your Word?
Have I accomplished Your will
     in sending me here?

Some nights when I can't sleep
     and my thoughts invade my room,
I relive these past two years
     in Cameroon.

I'm learning to be patient
    when I'm yelled at
    in a language I don't know.
I'm learning to love people
    who don't think or act
    or believe like me.
I'm learning to be peaceful
    amid rumors of a coup,
    during a time when all
    Americans living abroad
    have been threatened with death.
I'm learning to stand on Your Word
    that says Your healing power is the same
    yesterday, today, and forever.
I'm learning to trust You, Lord
    as I've never trusted You before.

Maybe I do understand.
You didn't send me here
    only for You,
    or them.
You also sent me here
    for me.

THE GIFT

Singleness is a gift,
    a box of freedom,
    a package of time.

Lord, I appreciate this present
    You have given me.

Other Living Books® Best-Sellers

THE ANGEL OF HIS PRESENCE by Grace Livingston Hill. This book captures the romance of John Wentworth Stanley and a beautiful young woman whose influence causes John to re-evaluate his well-laid plans for the future. 07-0047-3 $3.95.

ANSWERS by Josh McDowell and Don Stewart. In a question-and-answer format, the authors tackle sixty-five of the most-asked questions about the Bible, God, Jesus Christ, miracles, other religions, and creation. 07-0021-X $4.95.

BUILDING YOUR SELF-IMAGE by Josh McDowell. Here are practical answers to help you overcome your fears, anxieties, and lack of self-confidence. Learn how God's higher image of who you are can take root in your heart and mind. 07-1395-8 $4.95.

THE CHILD WITHIN by Mari Hanes. The author shares insights she gained from God's Word during her own pregnancy. She identifies areas of stress, offers concrete data about the birth process, and points to God's sure promises that he will "gently lead those that are with young." 07-0219-0 $3.95.

COME BEFORE WINTER AND SHARE MY HOPE by Charles R. Swindoll. A collection of brief vignettes offering hope and the assurance that adversity and despair are temporary setbacks we can overcome! 07-0477-0 $6.95.

DARE TO DISCIPLINE by James Dobson. A straightforward, plainly written discussion about building and maintaining parent/child relationships based upon love, respect, authority, and ultimate loyalty to God. 07-0522-X $4.95.

DR. DOBSON ANSWERS YOUR QUESTIONS by James Dobson. In this convenient reference book, renowned author Dr. James Dobson addresses heartfelt concerns on many topics including questions on marital relationships, infant care, child discipline, home management, and others. 07-0580-7 $5.95.

Other Living Books® Best-Sellers

FOR MEN ONLY edited by J. Allan Petersen. This book deals with topics of concern to every man: the business world, marriage, fathering, spiritual goals, and problems of living as a Christian in a secular world. 07-0892-X $4.95.

FOR WOMEN ONLY by Evelyn and J. Allan Petersen. Balanced, entertaining, diversified treatment of all aspects of womanhood. 07-0897-0 $5.95.

400 CREATIVE WAYS TO SAY I LOVE YOU by Alice Chapin. Perhaps the flame of love has almost died in your marriage. Maybe you have a good marriage that just needs a little "spark." Here is a book especially for the woman who wants to rekindle the flame of romance in her marriage, who wants creative, practical, useful ideas to show the man in her life that she cares. 07-0919-5 $3.95.

GIVERS, TAKERS, AND OTHER KINDS OF LOVERS by Josh McDowell and Paul Lewis. This book bypasses vague generalities about love and sex and gets right to the basic questions: Whatever happened to sexual freedom? What's true love like? Do men respond differently than women? If you're looking for straight answers about God's plan for love and sexuality, this book was written for you. 07-1031-2 $3.95.

HINDS' FEET ON HIGH PLACES by Hannah Hurnard. A classic allegory of a journey toward faith that has sold more than a million copies! 07-1429-6 $4.95.

HOW TO BE HAPPY THOUGH MARRIED by Tim LaHaye. One of America's most successful marriage counselors gives practical, proven advice for marital happiness. 07-1499-7 $4.95.

THE INTIMATE MARRIAGE by R. C. Sproul. The author focuses on biblical patterns of marriage and practical ways to develop intimacy. Discussion questions included at end of each chapter. 07-1610-8 $3.95.

JOHN, SON OF THUNDER by Ellen Gunderson Traylor. In this saga of adventure, romance, and discovery, travel with John—the disciple whom Jesus loved—down desert paths, through the courts of the Holy City, to the foot of the cross, as he leaves his luxury as a privileged son of Israel for the bitter hardship of his exile on Patmos. 07-1903-4 $5.95

Other Living Books® Best-Sellers

LIFE IS TREMENDOUS! by Charlie "Tremendous" Jones. Believing that enthusiasm makes the difference, Jones shows how anyone can be happy, involved, relevant, productive, healthy, and secure in the midst of a high-pressure, commercialized society. 07-2184-5 $3.95.

LORD, COULD YOU HURRY A LITTLE? by Ruth Harms Calkin. These prayer-poems from the heart of a godly woman trace the inner workings of the heart, following the rhythms of the day and seasons of the year with expectation and love. 07-3816-0 $3.95.

LORD, I KEEP RUNNING BACK TO YOU by Ruth Harms Calkin. In prayer-poems tinged with wonder, joy, humanness, and questioning, the author speaks for all of us who are groping and learning together what it means to be God's child. 07-3819-5 $3.95.

MORE THAN A CARPENTER by Josh McDowell. A hard-hitting book for people who are skeptical about Jesus' deity, his resurrection, and his claim on their lives. 07-4552-3 $3.95.

MOUNTAINS OF SPICES by Hannah Hurnard. Here is an allegory comparing the nine spices mentioned in the Song of Solomon to the nine fruits of the Spirit. A story of the glory of surrender by the author of *Hinds' Feet on High Places*. 07-4611-2 $4.95.

NOW IS YOUR TIME TO WIN by Dave Dean. In this true-life story, Dean shares how he locked into seven principles that enabled him to bounce back from failure to success. Read about successful men and women—from sports and entertainment celebrities to the ordinary people next door—and discover how you too can bounce back from failure to success! 07-4727-5 $3.95.

THE SECRET OF LOVING by Josh McDowell. McDowell explores the values and qualities that will help both single and married readers to be the right person for someone else. He offers a fresh perspective for evaluating and improving the reader's love life. 07-5845-5 $4.95.

THE STORY FROM THE BOOK. The full sweep of *The Book*'s contents in abridged, chronological form, giving the reader the "big picture" of the Bible. 07-6677-6 $4.95.

Other Living Books® Best-Sellers

STRIKE THE ORIGINAL MATCH by Charles Swindoll. Many couples ask: What do you do when the warm, passionate fire that once lit your marriage begins to wane? Here, Chuck Swindoll provides biblical steps for rekindling the fires of romance and building marital intimacy. 07-6445-5 $4.95.

SUCCESS: THE GLENN BLAND METHOD by Glenn Bland. The author shows how to set goals and make plans that really work. His ingredients of success include spiritual, financial, educational, and recreational balances. 07-6689-6 $4.95.

THROUGH GATES OF SPLENDOR by Elisabeth Elliot. This unforgettable story of five men who braved the Auca Indians has become one of the most famous missionary books of all times. 07-7151-6 $4.95.

WHAT WIVES WISH THEIR HUSBANDS KNEW ABOUT WOMEN by James Dobson. The best-selling author of *Dare to Discipline* and *The Strong-Willed Child* brings us this vital book that speaks to the unique emotional needs and aspirations of today's woman. An immensely practical, interesting guide. 07-7896-0 $4.95.

WHY YOU ACT THE WAY YOU DO by Tim LaHaye. Discover how your temperament affects your work, emotions, spiritual life, and relationships, and learn how to make improvements. 07-8212-7 $4.95.